DUDLEY SCHOOLS
LIBRARY SERVICE

KU-453-088

Schools Library and Information Services

S00000665582

Looking at
Small Mammals

Small Primates

Sally Morgan

Chrysalis Children's Books

First published in the UK in 2004
Ⓒ Chrysalis Children's Books
An imprint of Chrysalis Books Group PLC
The Chrysalis Building, Bramley Road,
London W10 6SP

Copyright © Chrysalis Books Group PLC 2004
Text copyright © Sally Morgan 2004

Editorial Manager: Joyce Bentley
Series editor: Debbie Foy
Editors: Clare Lewis, Joseph Fullman
Designer: Wladek Szechter
Picture researcher: Sally Morgan
Illustrations: Woody

All rights reserved. No part of this book
may be reproduced or utilized in any form
or by any means, electronic or mechanical,
including photocopying, recording or by
any information storage or retrieval system,
without written permission of the publisher,
except by a reviewer who may quote
passages in a review.

ISBN 1 84458 106 3

Printed in China.

10 9 8 7 6 5 4 3 2 1

British Library Cataloguing in Publication
Data for this book is available from the
British Library.

Picture acknowledgements:
Ecoscene: 27 Karl Ammann, 9B, 20 Michael
Gore, 15T, 17B Wayne Lawler, 1, 5T, 7T, 11B
Neeraj Mishra, 13B, 22 Sally Morgan, 8
Graham Neden, 5B Alan Towse, 19T
Papilio/Peter Bond, 19B Papilio/Paul Franklin,
12, 15B Papilio/Brian Cushing, 3, 4, 6, 10, 16
Papilio/Robert Gill, 7B, 9T, 14 Papilio/Bryan
Knox, 2, 11, 13T, 18, 21B, 23, 24, 25B, 26, 32
Papilio/Robert Pickett, 21T Robin Redfern.
Front Cover: TCR Wayne Lawler, TCL Neeraj
Mishra, BCL, CR, TL Papilio/Robert Gill,
TR Papilio/Robert Pickett. Back Cover:
TCR Wayne Lawler, TCL Neeraj Mishra,
TL Papilio/Robert Gill, TR Papilio/
Robert Pickett.
Frank Lane
Picture Agency:
25T J & C Sohns.
Geoff Jones: 17T.

Contents

L 47488

66 5582   SCH

J599.8

What are small primates?

Lemurs, slow lorises and monkeys are all primates. Humans are primates, too.

These ring-tailed lemurs are covered in fur like most mammals.

4

The slow loris climbs slowly through the trees, gripping with its hands and feet.

The primates belong to a group of animals called **mammals**. Most mammals have four legs and are covered in hair.

They give birth to live young. Young mammals feed on their mother's milk for the first months of their lives.

Baby primates keep close to their mother for protection and for food.

The primate family

Lemurs have hands that can pick up food and other objects.

Most small primates live in trees. They have long arms and legs, each with five fingers or toes. They can pick things up with their hands and feet.

The golden leaf monkey has two forward-pointing eyes that can judge distances.

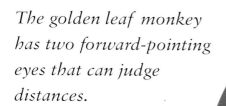

Primates have a large brain and are intelligent animals. They also have well developed senses.

The indri, a type of lemur, uses its sharp eyes and good sense of hearing as it moves around the forest.

7

Where do small primates live?

Small primates are found in southern Asia, Africa and South America but not in Australia or the colder parts of the world such as Northern Europe and North America.

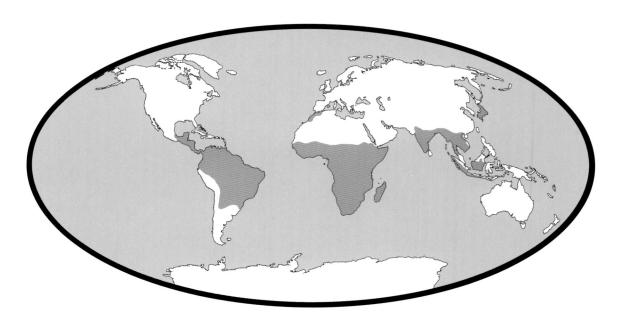

The areas shaded in pink on this map of the world show where small primates live.

The brown mouse lemur is one of the smallest primates.

Lemurs are only found on the island of Madagascar. Madagascar lies off the east coast of Africa. Primates live mostly in forests.

Ring-tailed lemurs are named after the black and white markings on their long tails.

Lemurs, tarsiers and bush babies

These primates have a dog-like face with large, round eyes. They have nails on their fingers and toes, except for a claw on their second toe.

Ring-tailed lemurs are often seen sitting in the sun.

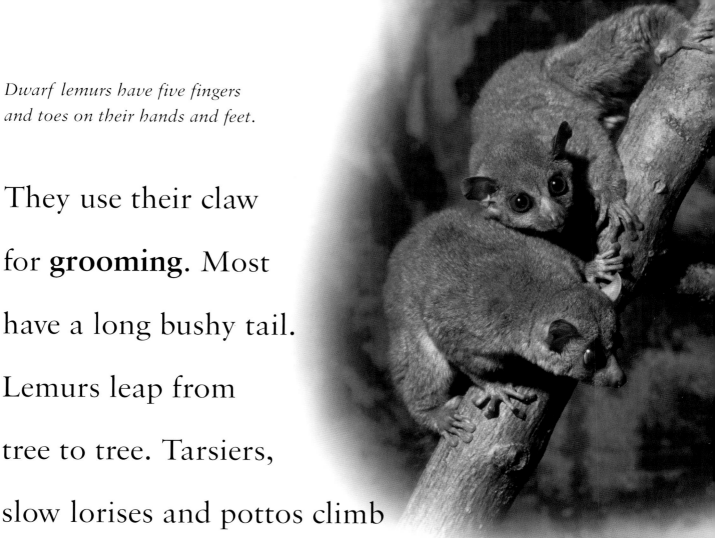

Dwarf lemurs have five fingers and toes on their hands and feet.

They use their claw for **grooming**. Most have a long bushy tail. Lemurs leap from tree to tree. Tarsiers, slow lorises and pottos climb slowly along the branches.

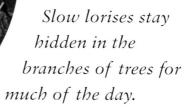

Slow lorises stay hidden in the branches of trees for much of the day.

Monkeys

Monkeys have a flattened chest and a short, flat face. They have four large, sharp teeth at the front of their mouth called **canines**. Monkeys have long limbs.

The male proboscis monkey has a long droopy nose.

The golden lion tamarin has a magnificent golden mane around its head and shoulders.

Their legs are slightly longer than their arms. Their hands can grip objects and are used for picking up food and grooming. Most monkeys have a long tail, too.

The baboon has four long legs and a long tail.

What do small primates eat?

Some small primates are **herbivores**. This means that they eat only plant foods such as leaves, nuts and fruits. They may lick **nectar** from flowers.

A ring-tailed lemur climbs through the trees looking for fruit.

These macaque monkeys are combing the undergrowth in search of food.

Other primates are **omnivores** as they eat both plant and animal foods such as insects. Some of the capuchin monkeys also eat lizards and frogs. Tarsiers are **carnivores** as they eat just meat.

The crown lemur is an herbivore, feeding on leaves and fruits.

15

Finding food

Many small primates are **nocturnal**. This means that they sleep during the day and come out at night to feed. They have good senses, especially sight and smell.

The brown eyes of this crown lemur catch the light at night.

This family of ring-tailed lemurs has pulled down a branch to reach the leaves and fruits.

Nocturnal primates need large eyes to help them see in the dark. Lemurs have an excellent sense of smell and this helps them to find ripe fruit or insects hidden under the bark of trees.

This macaque comes out during the day to search for food.

17

Getting around

The prehensile tail of this spider monkey is wrapped around a branch, helping the monkey to move through the trees.

Most small primates live in trees. Their eyes point forwards so that they can judge distances. This is important as they have to climb trees and jump from branch to branch. Most small primates have a long tail that helps them to balance as they move through the trees.

*A proboscis monkey
travels through the forest
by leaping from tree to tree.*

Some primates have a **prehensile** tail which acts like a fifth limb as it can wrap itself around branches and grip.

*Squirrel monkeys move
through the trees by jumping
from branch to branch.*

19

Living together

A few small primates live on their own, but most live together in a group. A group usually consists of females and their young, with one or two males. Some groups are large with more than 50 individuals.

A macaque grooms the fur around the face of another in its group.

Baboons live in large groups called troops.

Primates like to groom each other. They pick through each other's fur to clean it. This helps to keep the group together. The primates move through the trees as a group, calling to each other as they hunt for food.

The booming call of the male howler monkey carries far through the forest.

Life cycle

A young baboon relies on its mother for food.

Primates give birth to a single baby. Sometimes they have twins. The mother feeds her baby with milk for the first months of its life. She usually carries it around as she moves through the trees.

The smallest primates live for about 15 years in the wild. The larger monkeys may live to between 25 and 30 years.

A female baboon holds her baby close to her to clean it.

Looking after their young

Small primates look after their young. They feed and protect them.

A baby ring-tailed lemur clambers over its mother and plays with her.

24

Young macaque monkeys learn by watching the adults in their group.

The youngsters spend much of their time playing and exploring with other youngsters in the group. They learn what foods are safe to eat.

Young colobus monkeys must learn how to move through the trees and find food.

Large primates

Small primates have some large relatives.

The largest primates are the apes – orang utans, gibbons, chimpanzees, gorillas and humans.

This adult male gorilla is called a 'silverback' because of the silver-coloured fur over his back.

Orang utans are large apes with red hair. They live alone in the forests of South East Asia.

A male gorilla can weigh more than 160 kg, a thousand times heavier than a marmoset or bush baby. Apes have no tail and their arms are longer than their legs. They live in forests too. They feed on a mixed diet of plants and animals.

Investigate!

Hands and feet

Your own hand is similar to the hand of a small primate. Look at your hand. See how your thumb sticks out at an angle to your fingers. Watch how you pick up something and how your thumb grips the object. Look at your feet. Find out how your foot differs to that of a monkey or a lemur.

Look at how your thumb and fingers are positioned on your hand.

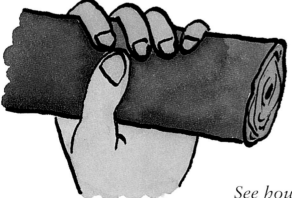

See how your thumb and fingers work together to grip an object.

Using our teeth

Our teeth are similar to the teeth of other primates. When you eat something, like an apple for example, try and work out which teeth you use to bite the food and which you use to chew it.

Look at the bite marks that your teeth leave behind after you bite off a mouthful of food.

Finding out more

Many zoos and wildlife parks keep small primates, especially monkeys. Here you will be able to watch the primates and see how they eat, pick things up, move around and communicate with each other. You can learn more about small primates by reading books and searching on the Internet.

Small primate facts

✓ The tiny mouse lemur weighs only 55g!

✓ The western tarsier can turn its head right around to look backwards!

✓ The bush baby sprays its urine over its own feet. As it walks along tree branches it leaves a trail of smells which the bush baby can follow to find its way back.

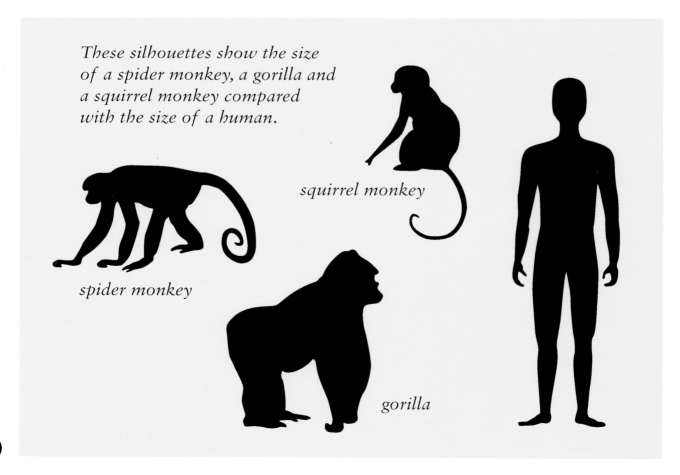

These silhouettes show the size of a spider monkey, a gorilla and a squirrel monkey compared with the size of a human.

squirrel monkey

spider monkey

gorilla

Glossary

canine A large tooth near the front of the mouth. Most mammals have four canine teeth.

carnivore A type of mammal that eats other animals.

grooming The cleaning of fur, removing dirt and small animals such as fleas and ticks.

herbivore An animal that eats only plant foods such as leaves, fruit and roots.

mammal An animal that feeds their young milk and is covered in fur.

nectar The sugary liquid produced by many flowers.

nocturnal Active at night, asleep during the day.

omnivore An animal that eats a variety of plant and animal foods.

prehensile (tail) A tail that is capable of grasping.

Index